Delaney
Street
Press

A Wee Bit of
Irish Wisdom

A Wee Bit of
Irish Wisdom

By Jim Gallery

DELANEY STREET PRESS
Nashville, TN (800)-256-8584

ISBN 1-58334-072-6

The ideas expressed in this book are not, in all cases, exact quotations, as some have been edited for clarity and brevity. In all cases, the author has attempted to maintain the speaker's original intent. In some cases, material for this book was obtained from secondary sources, primarily print media. While every effort was made to ensure the accuracy of these sources, the accuracy cannot be guaranteed. For additions, deletions, corrections or clari-fications in future editions of this text, please write DELANEY STREET PRESS.

Cover Design by Bart Dawson
Typesetting & Page Layout by Sue Gerdes
Printed in the United States of America
1 2 3 4 5 6 7 8 9 10 • 00 01 02 03

ACKNOWLEDGMENTS

The author gratefully acknowledges the helpful support of Eloise Gallery, Criswell Freeman, and the great folks at Delaney Street Press and Walnut Grove.

For Ron McMedlin
Who embodies the best
of Irish virtues

Table of Contents

God made the grass, the air and the rain; and the grass, the air and the rain made the Irish; and the Irish turned the grass, the air and the rain back to God.

Sean O'Faolain

Introduction

It is a true saying that most everyone is Irish on St. Patrick's Day. Rainbows, leprechauns, the Blarney Stone, and Shamrocks evoke the child-like wonder inside all of us.

The wisdom in this book — though only a wee bit in quantity — is abundant in quality. These pages are intended to provoke thoughtful reflection, warm feelings for family and friends, and an appreciation for the magic which comes from the Emerald Isle.

Proverbs, sayings, toasts, blessings, and quotations can brighten any reader's day. So take a few moments to find your 'pot-o-gold' in these words of Irish wisdom.

1

Doing the Right Thing

Character is forged by right action built upon a foundation of strong faith. Some people would stereotype the Irish as "characters." But the truth of the matter is that the Irish have character which comes from powerful conviction.

As Father Flanagan noted, "Character is formed by doing the thing we are supposed to do, when it should be done, whether we feel like doing it or not." So when in doubt, do the right thing, whether you feel like it or not. And while you're at it, turn the page and partake in a few Irish insights that, if taken to heart, will never fail you.

Without God
at the beginning
there can only
be confusion
at the end.

Father Flanagan

Man is born broken.
        He lives by mending.
    The grace of God is the glue.

Eugene O'Neill

We look for God as though
        he is not already here.

Merritt Malloy

When man makes God,
        there is no God.

Eugene O'Neill

Without religious faith there
can be no lasting enthusiasm.
Man cannot lift himself by tugging
at his own bootstraps.
Father Flanagan

Faith and work make
a triumphant combination.
Father Flanagan

Character is better than wealth.

Irish Saying

Character is the sum
of the choices that a
human being makes
under pressure.

Robert McKee

Great crises produce
great men and great
deeds of courage.

John Kennedy

Let your courage
guide your future.
Finlay McKenna

No man is rich enough to buy back
his own past.

Oscar Wilde

Truth lies in the cellar;
error on the doorstep.

Austin O'Malley

It is twice as hard to crush a half-truth
as a whole lie.

Austin O'Malley

Never confuse
a single mistake
with a final
mistake.

F. Scott Fitzgerald

2

The Luck of the Irish

Shamrocks and the "luck of the Irish" are nice things to think about. Luck and good fortune are desired by all. But, the truth is revealed in an old Irish proverb: "There is no luck except where there is discipline."

John Kennedy, a man of Irish heritage and work ethic, reflected, "Things do not happen. They are made to happen." Kennedy understood that good fortune is seldom a matter of good luck — it is more often a matter of good work.

So take a few moments to enjoy these sayings about Irish luck and the hard work that makes it possible. Then go out and start making some good luck of your own.

If you are lucky
enough to be Irish,
you're lucky enough.

Grace Boyle

Wherever you go
and whatever you do,
May the luck of the
Irish be there with you.

Irish Blessing

There is a silent
dignity, a fundamental
usefulness, and a
primeval necessity
in work.

Father Flanagan

Laziness is a heavy load.

Irish Proverb

Luck means the long nights you have
devoted to work. Luck means the
appointments you have never failed
to keep; the trains you have never
failed to catch.

Max O'Rell

Look at your choices; pick
the best one, then go with it.

Pat Riley

The days you work are the best days.

Georgia O'Keefe

The work praises
the man.
Irish Proverb

A goal is a dream
with a deadline.
Harvey MacKay

The work is
a picture of
the man.
Irish Proverb

If your play interrupts your work, you're healthy. If work interrupts your play, you're broke.

James (Big Jim) O'Hara

You always pass failure
on the way to success.

Mickey Rooney

The higher the ideal the more work is required to accomplish it. Do not expect to become a great success in life if you are not willing to work for it.

Father Flanagan

Let us go forth asking His help and His blessing, but knowing that here on earth, God's work must truly be our own.

John Kennedy

Your luck is how you treat people.
Bridget O'Donnell

She didn't know it couldn't be done,
so she went ahead and did it.
Bridget O'Donnell

Man does not live
as he thinks; he
thinks as he lives.

Reverend Vaughan Quinn

May your pockets
be heavy and your heart
be light; May good luck
pursue you morning
and night.

Irish Toast

3

Impassioned Living

When asked about the Irish character, Edna O'Brien once observed, "Look at the trees of Ireland: maimed, stark and misshapen, but ferociously tenacious."

The Irish have been stereotyped as tempestuous spirits, and this characterization is undoubtedly accurate in many cases. But, along with the notoriously quick Irish temper comes a deep passion for life. Sons and daughters of the Emerald Isle live life to the full.

The following words encourage us to leave the mediocre behind and join those wise Irish souls who make each day a joyous exercise in impassioned living.

The Irish, with their glowing hearts, are needed in this age.

Lydia Maria Child

Only those who dare to
fail miserably
can achieve greatly.
Robert Kennedy

Life is half-spent
before we know
what it is.

Irish Proverb

We need above all
to learn again to believe
in the possibility of
nobility of spirit
in ourselves.

Eugene O'Neill

Don't let other people tell you
what you want.

Pat Riley

The important thing is to learn a lesson
even though you lose.

John McEnroe

God never shuts one door
    unless He opens another.
                          Irish Proverb

One man with a dream, at pleasure,
  Shall go forth and conquer a crown....
        Arthur William Edgar O'Shaughnessy

The world belongs
to the enthusiast
who keeps his cool.
William McFee

Success is not so much achievement as achieving. Refuse to join the cautious crowd that plays not to lose, play to win.
David J. Mahoney

A tie is like kissing your sister.
Duffy Daugherty

If fate means you to lose,
give him a good fight anyhow.
William McFee

Sometimes it's risky
not to take a risk.

Harvey MacKay

4

Love, Joy, and Laughter

Wise Irishmen understand that a well-lived life is one of love, joy, and laughter. The late sports writer Jim Murray observed, "We Irishmen are banking heavily on the fact that God has a sense of humor." God does.

The following samples of Irish wisdom remind us that the essence of life is found not in things, but in ourselves. When we smile at life, life smiles back. And as insightful Irish men and women know all too well, each day is a priceless opportunity to share laughter and love.

When Irish eyes are smiling,
Sure it's like a morning spring.
In the lilt of Irish laughter
You can hear the angels sing.
When Irish hearts are happy,
All the world seems bright and gay.
And when Irish eyes are smiling,
They'll steal your heart away!

Irish Folk Song

May your home be filled with laughter,
May your pockets be filled with gold,
And may you have all the happiness
Your Irish heart can hold.

Irish Blessing

Don't hurry. Don't worry. You're only here for a short visit. So don't forget to stop and smell the roses.

Walter Hagen

Many people think
they are taking life
seriously when they
are only taking
themselves seriously.

Joseph T. O'Callahan

Birds sing after the storm. Why shouldn't we?

Rose Fitzgerald Kennedy

Music, melody, and rhythm find their way into the secret places of the soul, radiating joy.

Father Flanagan

For me, singing sad songs often has
a way of healing a situation. It gets the
hurt out in the open — into the light,
out of the darkness.

Reba McEntire

There is wisdom in the habit of looking
at the bright side of life.

Father Flanagan

In happiness brought
to others, our own
happiness is reflected.
Father Flanagan

A man that can't laugh
at himself should be
given a mirror.

Irish Saying

The best way to get a husband to do anything is to suggest that perhaps he is too old to do it.

Shirley MacLaine

Courtship is a time during which the girl decides whether she can do better or not.

Irish Saying

The Irish don't know what they want
and are prepared to fight to the death
to get it.

Sidney Littlewood

God created whiskey so the Irish
would not conquer the world.

Irish Saying

Hard work never killed anybody,
but why take the chance?

Charlie McCarthy

It is not a secret if it is known
by three people.

Irish Proverb

I can resist everything
but temptation.

Oscar Wilde

The light heart
lives long.

Irish Proverb

May your heart
be warm and happy
With the lilt of
Irish laughter
Everyday in every way
And forever and
ever after.

Irish Blessing

5

A Friend Forever

The Irish love their family and their friends. Loyalty and a tenacious commitment to loved ones are the hallmarks of Irish relationships.

So raise a toast, read a quote, and take a few moments to contemplate that great and wonderful gift: enduring friendships.

May you always have
these blessings…
A soft breeze when
summer comes,
A warm fireside
in winter,
And always the warm,
soft smile of a friend.

Irish Blessing

Here's to absent friends and
   here's twice to absent enemies.

Irish Toast

Forsake not a friend of many years
   for the acquaintance of a day.

Irish Saying

A friend's eye is
a good mirror.
Irish Proverb

Better the coldness
of a friend than
the sweetness of
an enemy.

Irish Saying

May you always have work
for your hands to do.
May your pockets always hold
a coin or two.
May the sun shine bright
on your window pane.
May the rainbow be certain
to follow each rain.
May the hand of a friend
always be near you
and may God fill your heart
with gladness to cheer you.

Irish Toast

May your home always be too small
to hold all of your friends.
Irish Blessing

May the roof above us never fall in,
And may the friends gathered below it
never fall out.
Irish Blessing

The first rule of orphanages and
Irish families is there's always room
for one more.
Father Frances Mulcahy (M*A*S*H)

May your neighbors respect you,
Trouble neglect you,
The angels protect you,
And heaven accept you.

Irish Blessing

May your right hand always be
stretched out in friendship
And never in want.

Irish Blessing

There is no strength
without unity.

Irish Proverb

The older the fiddle
the sweeter the tune.
Irish Proverb

The old believe everything;
   the middle age suspect everything;
      the young know everything.

Oscar Wilde

Age is honorable and youth is noble.

Irish Proverb

A young person should never be made
to feel that no great thing is expected
      of him or her.

Father Flanagan

You can stroke people with words.

F. Scott Fitzgerald

6

Observations About Life

Like any ancient and proud culture, the Irish people have numerous sayings that instruct us how to live happy and productive lives. Please feel free to enjoy the following life lessons from the Emerald Isle.

Let your anger set with
the sun and not rise
again with it.

Irish Saying

Listen to the sound of the river,
    and you will get a trout.
                                    Irish Proverb

Put silk on a goat, and it is still a goat.
                                    Irish Proverb

Time is a great storyteller.
                                    Irish Proverb

If a man fools me once, shame on him.
  If he fools me twice, shame on me.
Irish Saying

The well fed does not
    understand the lean.
Irish Proverb

The wearer best knows
    where the shoe pinches.
Irish Proverb

The time to repair
the roof is when
the sun is shining.

John Kennedy

It is a long road
that has no turning.
Irish Proverb

Man's loneliness is but
his fear of life.

Eugene O'Neill

A silent mouth is melodious.
Irish Proverb

It is as foolish to let a fool kiss you
as it is to let a kiss fool you.
Irish Saying

If you keep your mouth shut,
you will never put your foot in it.
Austin O'Malley

Good as drink is, it ends in thirst.

Irish Proverb

Leave the table hungry.
Leave the bed sleepy.

Old Irish recipe for long life

The mills of God
grind slowly, but
they grind finely.
Irish Proverb

7

Irish Toasts

Everyone likes to be celebrated. The Irish do it well. Volumes have been written on Irish toasts. The following examples of Irish toast-making remind us that Irishmen celebrate best, because they truly celebrate each other. So feel free to use these toasts to encourage or entertain a friend or a loved one — it's the Irish way.

These things I warmly
wish for you —
Someone to love,
Some work to do,
A bit o' sun
A bit o' cheer
And a guardian angel
Always near.

Irish Toast

May you be across Heaven's threshold
before the old boy knows you are dead.

Irish Toast

In the New Year, may your right hand
always be stretched out in friendship
and never in want.

Irish Toast

May you live to be a hundred years,
with one extra year to repent.

Irish Toast

May the Lord
keep you in his hand
and never close his fist
too tight.

Irish Toast

May you live
as long as you want,
and never want
as long as you live.

Irish Toast

May the Irish hills
caress you.
May her lakes and rivers
bless you.
May the luck of the
Irish enfold you.
May the blessings
of Saint Patrick
behold you.

Irish Toast

May peace and plenty be the first
to lift the latch on your door,
And happiness be guided to your home
by the candle of Christmas.

Irish Toast

May you have warm words
on a cold evening,
A full moon on a dark night,
And the road downhill
all the way to your door.

Irish Toast

May the saddest day
of your future be
no worse than
the happiest day
of your past.

Irish Toast

May God grant you
many years to live,
for sure he must be
knowing the earth has
angels all too few and
heaven is overflowing.

Irish Toast

May your neighbors
respect you,
Trouble neglect you,
The angels protect you,
And heaven accept you.

Irish Toast

8

Blessings

The world would be a better place with more kind words. The world would be a changed place with less criticism and more praise.

The blessing is the Irish contribution to a lovelier, kinder, happier world. These blessings, courtesy of the Emerald Isle, should be taken to heart and then passed on to others.

May the blessings
of each day be
the blessings you
need most.

Irish Blessing

For each petal on the shamrock
    This brings a wish your way—
Good health, good luck, and happiness
    For today and every day.
          Irish Blessing

May your blessings outnumber
    The shamrocks that grow,
And may trouble avoid you
    Wherever you go.
          Irish Blessing

May your troubles be less
　　And your blessings be more.
　　And nothing but happiness
　　Come through your door.

Irish Blessing

May the raindrops fall lightly
　　　　on your brow;
May the soft winds freshen your spirit;
May the sunshine brighten your heart;
　　May the burdens of the day rest
　　　　lightly upon you;
And may God enfold you in the mantle
　　　　of His love.

Irish Blessing

Lucky stars above you,
Sunshine on your way,
Many friends
to love you,
Joy in work and play,
Laughter to outweigh
each care,
In your heart a song,
And gladness
waiting everywhere
All your whole life long!

Irish Blessing

May you have
the hindsight to know
where you've been,
The foresight to know
where you're going,
And the insight to know
when you're going
too far.

Irish Blessing

May you never
forget what is worth
remembering, or
remember what
is best forgotten.

Irish Blessing

9

A Few Facts About Ireland

Ireland boasts a rich history and a colorful heritage. A detailed history of the Emerald Isle is beyond the scope of this wee little book. But, perhaps a few facts about Ireland will spark a desire to learn more. Thus, we conclude with a small sampling of Irish information. Enjoy!

At any place on the Emerald Isle,
  you are only a maximum of seventy
    miles from the sea.

Ireland is known as the Emerald Isle,
  because of the lush greenery resulting
from almost daily rains. These daily rains
  also produce magical rainbows.

The Shamrock is regarded as the national plant of Ireland. Legend has it that St. Patrick used the Shamrock to illustrate the mystery of the Trinity.

Leprechauns supposedly possess
secret knowledge resulting in
the ability to find hidden gold.

You must keep your eyes on the
leprechaun. If you do, he will lead you
to a pot of gold. But, if you take your
eyes off him for even a second,
he will disappear.

The Blarney Stone is located in the tower of Blarney Castle in County Cork. A kiss of the Blarney Stone results in a gift of speaking, or some would say, the gift of gab.

St. Patrick was born in Scotland, not Ireland. But, as a young boy, he was sold into slavery in Ireland. His missionary zeal led to the Christian conversion of many. The banishment of snakes from the Emerald Isle is one of many legends attributed to him.

Hundreds of years ago, Belfast was known as the linen-making capital of the world. Today, Ireland is still recognized for its fine linen.

Oscar Wilde is famous for his novels and his plays. But, this Irishman also led the art community in a movement that advocated "art for art's sake."

One of Ireland's most famous writers is the playwright George Bernard Shaw, who won the Nobel Prize in Literature in 1925.

His parents were English. But, Jonathan Swift was born in Dublin and educated in Ireland. Thus, the Emerald Isle can claim as its own the author of *Gulliver's Travels*.

Ireland is home to many ancient castles. For the most part, these buildings were not elegant homes for Irish royalty; instead, castles were built in order to provide security for villages and clans.

And in conclusion...

May you have all the
happiness and luck that
life can hold —
And at the end of all
your rainbows may
you find a pot of gold.

Irish Blessing

Sources

About the Author

Jim Gallery lives and writes in Middle Tennessee. He serves as Coordinating Publisher for both Walnut Grove Press and Delaney Street Press. In addition, Jim is a sought-after speaker and lecturer. He is a graduate of the University of South Florida and the New Orleans Baptist Theological Seminary. He is the father of two children.

About
DELANEY STREET PRESS

DELANEY STREET PRESS publishes books designed to inspire and entertain readers of all ages. DELANEY STREET books are distributed by WALNUT GROVE PRESS. For more information, please call 1-800-256-8584.

If you enjoyed this book,
you're sure to enjoy other titles
from Delaney Street Press.
For more information,
please call:

1-800-256-8584